SAM ITA | PAUL FRASCO

Photography by Dario Canova

TUTTLE Publishing

Tokyo | Rutland, Vermont | Singapore

Contents

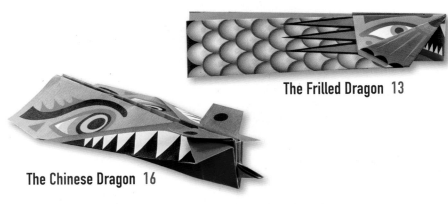

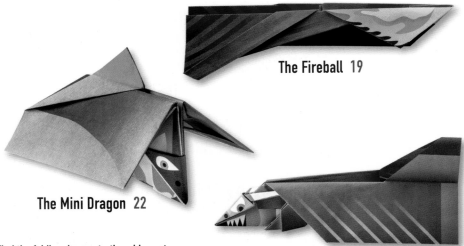

Find the folding demonstration videos at
www.tuttlepublishing.com/flying-dragons-paper-airplane-kit-demos

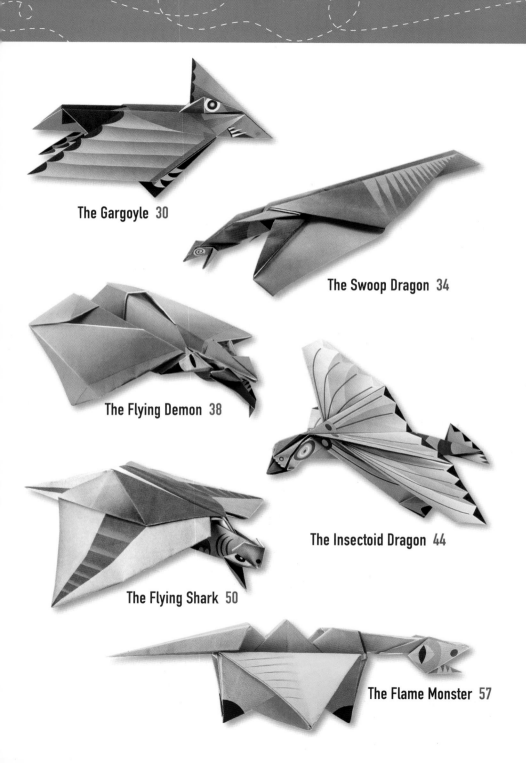

Introduction

This kit is a follow-up to my *Next Generation Paper Airplanes Kit*. One plane from that kit, "The Gremlin," gave me the idea to create an entire collection of models, in the form of flying creatures. It was hard enough to come up with original models that actually flew well. This kit's dragon theme added another hurdle, and an awfully high one, at that. Would it prove to be a fool's errand? I'd find out soon enough.

Luckily, I had help. After carefully considering it for a few seconds, my good friend, and occasional collaborator, Paul Frasco agreed to co-author this book. He is an origami expert, who had designed numerous fantasy creature models.

I see origami as a language. It can be used to describe anything. But it requires skill and imagination to articulate. Origami can be poetry—and what is more poetic than flight?

A satisfying model involves not only precision and logic, but an element of magic. At some point, the paper completely transforms, like an egg hatching, a flower blooming or a butterfly emerging from its cocoon. Even if you are familiar enough with origami to recognize the mechanics of the transformation, there is something very enjoyable about watching the story unfold. Or in this case, literally, the reverse.

The story of this book begins with Paul folding beautiful dragons with well-articulated legs, wings, claws, horns, tails and eyelids. The problem was that they were difficult to fold, and too dense to fly well. Conversely, my earliest attempts flew better, and were easier to fold, but hardly resembled dragons.

Working with paper is a struggle. After working with it for so many years, I am still surprised by what it will agree to do, and what it won't. Convincing it to take a form is at once enjoyable, challenging and frustrating. It can be a bit like teaching a bright, but stubborn child.

I believe our efforts on the book paid off nicely. We managed to invent a wide variety of flying dragons. Each with a unique form, flying style and personality. This book begins with simpler, easier to fold models, and incrementally advances to the more sophisticated ones. As they get more complicated, they become smaller and more compact, like today's modern lizard, the basis of so many fantasy creatures.

A lot of hard work went into developing these models. We had a lot of fun, too. We hope that folding these dragons is as much of an adventure for you as it has been for us.

—Sam Ita

Folding Instructions

STOP

Naturally, you may want to skip the instructions and jump right into the fun stuff. That is perfectly understandable, but you should consider that these instructions can prevent a good deal of frustration, and help you fold much better planes. I encourage you to get a few sheets of origami paper and do the following folds. Don't worry, we'll go slowly.

Dashed lines indicate **Valley Folds**. This means that the crease ends up at the bottom of the completed fold. The arrow indicates the direction that the paper should be folded.

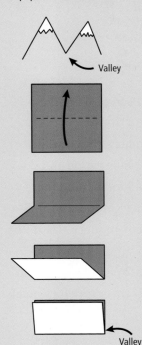

Mountain Folds go the other way. They are usually represented by a line of dots and dashes. This means that the crease ends up on top, once the fold is complete. I think of the dots as peaks of mountains.

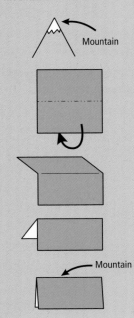

A **Double Headed Arrow** means you need to fold and unfold. This weakens the paper slightly, leaving a crease.

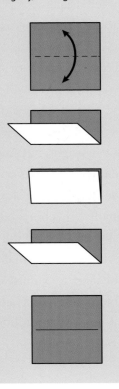

The **Inside Reverse Fold** is also very common.

It usually follows a crease, created by a previous fold and unfold.

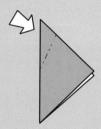

Now, push against the center, creating mountain folds on both sides.

The completed **Inside Reverse Fold**.

The **Waterbomb Base** is an important starting point.

Mountain fold and unfold diagonally.

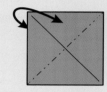

And again, in the other direction.

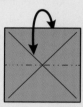

This will leave you with creases that form an "X." Fold in half, away from you.

Push in the corners.

The completed **Waterbomb Base**.

The **Squash Fold** is common in origami and paper planes.

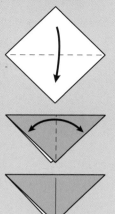

The **Outlined Arrow** means "push." It means to apply pressure to the paper along a given path. In this case, it refolds a previous valley fold, while creating two new mountain folds.

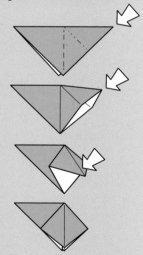

The completed **Squash Fold**. Continue on the following page to form the **Square Base**.

Turn the paper over.

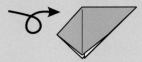

And do the same thing on the other side.

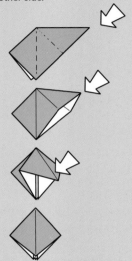

The completed **Square Base**.

The **Swivel Fold** involves moving a flap of paper around a set point, then resquashing in another position. This fold begins with the Square Base.

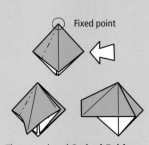

The completed **Swivel Fold**.

The **Petal Fold** can begin with a Square Base. There is more than one way to perform this sequence.

Fold the bottom edges in to the center. Unfold.

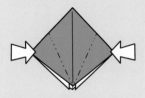

Push in the flaps and reverse the creases.

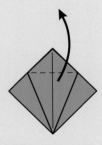

Fold the flap up.

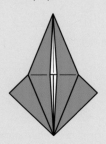

The completed **Petal Fold**.

The **Frog Fold** can also begin with a Square Base.

Fold a single flap half way up.

Squash fold the flap.

Fold the bottom edges in to the center. Unfold.

Refold the bottom creases, while pulling up the center of the top layer to perform a squash fold at each side.

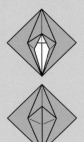

The completed **Frog Fold**.

Paper Airplane Mastery Tips

Understanding a few key points will help your dragons fly better. A little origami skill, and a little knowledge of paper airplanes will come in handy. There is a lot overlap between the two. The first ingredient is clean, precise folding. How do you achieve this? Well, start with clean, dry hands. While you're folding, take your time, breathe and relax. The rest comes with experience. Another important, somewhat contradictory concept is *slack*. This can help with origami in general, but it is an asset to paper planes in particular. Slack refers to the space you leave between edges. Heavier paper requires more slack. In any case, the amount is small, a millimeter at most. Leaving slack is important, because it gives you space to fold between the edges.

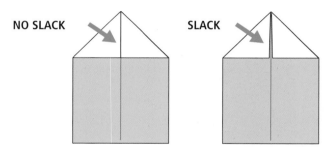

NO SLACK   **SLACK**

Thrust is forward force. In the case of paper planes, it comes entirely from the pilot's arm. Keep in mind, this thrust is never perfectly straight. Weight in the nose allows more thrust to be applied.

THRUST

LIFT

The path of air over the wings can convert some of the thrust to lift. However, too much lift, too far forward, will cause the plane to stall and fall backwards.

DRAG

Drag is from friction created by air resistance. Drag slows the plane, allowing gravity to pull it down. Locks and simple design can help minimize drag.

GRAVITY

What goes up must come down. But paper planes are light enough to resist gravity for at least a little while.

Front / Rear View

If you were to look at a cross section of a dart-style paper airplane, it would look something like the diagrams below. Notice how, in the first diagram, the fuselage is not locked, so it tends to hang wide open.

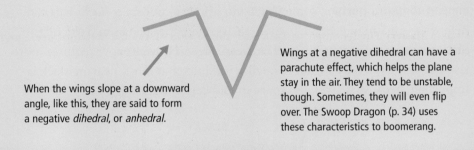

When the wings slope at a downward angle, like this, they are said to form a negative *dihedral*, or *anhedral*.

Wings at a negative dihedral can have a parachute effect, which helps the plane stay in the air. They tend to be unstable, though. Sometimes, they will even flip over. The Swoop Dragon (p. 34) uses these characteristics to boomerang.

Now, let's compare this to a locked fuselage.

Here, the wings form a positive dihedral, granting the model much greater stability.

The loose lock on the fuselage reduces drag, without reducing the wing surface area.

The tips of the wings can be folded up or down to create winglets. Winglets help to further stabilize the aircraft, strengthen, and in some cases, lock the wings. The trade-off being that they reduce the wing surface area.

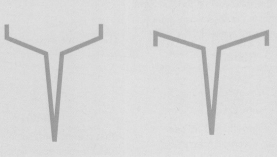

Quetzalcoatl (The Feathered Serpent)

The easiest dragon to fold happens to have the most difficult name to pronounce. The Quetzalcoatl, or "feathered serpent," is a mythological creature, originally from ancient Mesoamerica. It has taken various forms and meanings across civilizations. Typically associated with the planet Venus, Quetzalcoatl guarded the boundary between earth and sky. This version of Quetzalcoatl has large wings and glides easily.

Dragon Mastery Tip: Its simple design makes this dragon well suited for adjustment and customization. Set the wings at an upward angle for added stability.

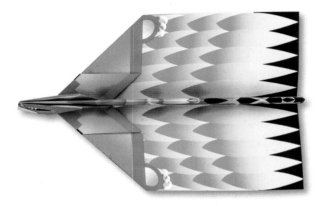

1

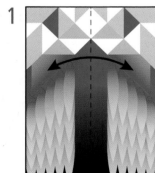

Begin with the back side up, in vertical orientation. Valley fold and unfold, edge to edge.

2

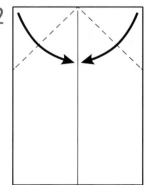

Fold the top edges to the center.

3

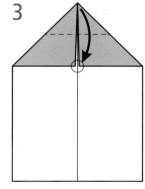

Fold down the top corner to the other corners.

4

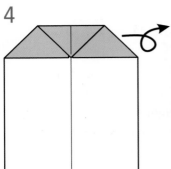

Turn over.

5

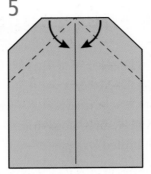

Valley fold the top edges inward to the center line.

6

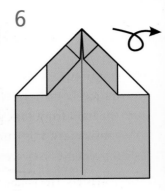

Turn over.

7

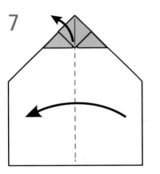

Valley fold in half, while pulling out the bottom corner of the top square.

8

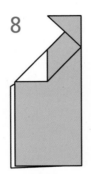

Rotate 90°.

9

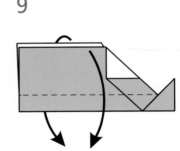

Fold the wings down.

10

Adjust the wings and launch.

The Frilled Dragon

Unlike its more famous running cousin, the Frilled Dragon has a solid, boxy appearance. In its jungle habitat, its stubby wings allow it to glide from tree to tree. The tight front lock gives it a good amount of weight in the front, and helps it fly consistently. It is a uniquely amphibious dragon, with a scaly body and a taste for seafood. Beware the Frilled Dragon! It's more than just a scary face.

Dragon Mastery Tip: Folding the tips of the wings, technically called winglets, helps paper dragons and planes glide better, by trapping more air under them. Winglets also serve to add stability and strength to the wings.

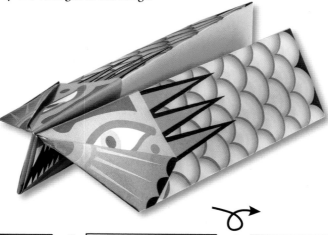

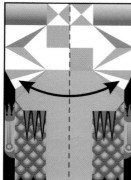

1

Begin with back side up, in vertical orientation. Valley Fold and unfold, edge to edge.

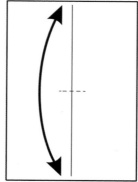

2

Fold the top edge to the bottom. Pinch the center to make a mark. Turn over.

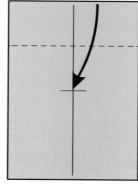

3

Valley fold the top edge to the pinch mark.

4

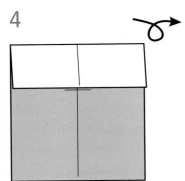

Turn over.

5

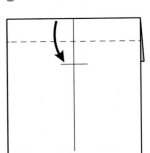

Valley fold the top edge to the pinch mark.

6

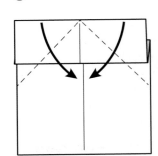

Fold the top edges to the center line, through all the layers.

7

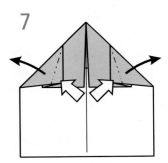

Squash fold the edges outward.

8

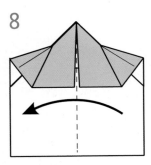

Valley fold in half.

9

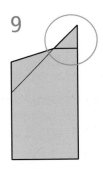

Zoom in.

10

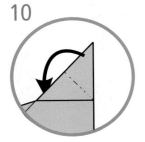

Mountain fold the top triangle.

11

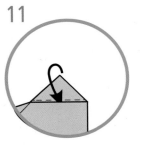

Valley fold and tuck in.

12

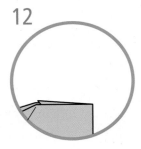

The lock is complete. Zoom out.

13

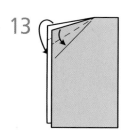

Valley fold both edges to the creases. Rotate 90°.

14

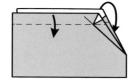

Valley fold the winglets down.

15

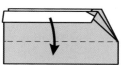

Fold the wing down, parallel to the bottom.

16

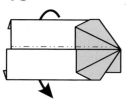

Fold the other wing down to match. The Frilled Dragon is ready to fly.

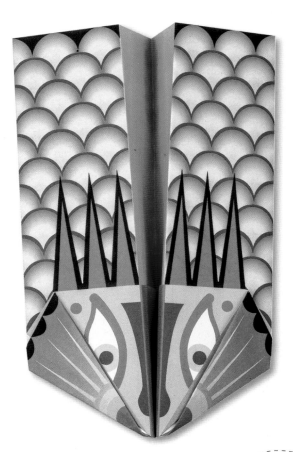

The Chinese Dragon

Dragons have existed in Chinese mythology since ancient times. To celebrate the Lunar New Year, performers use bamboo poles to control a giant dragon puppet. It is wonderful to watch. This flying version was inspired by the dancing dragon's head. It flies much like a solid, front-weighted dart, with flaring nostrils.

Dragon Mastery Tip: If necessary, the tips of the nostrils can be tucked in to reduce drag (step 19). This model uses a Frog Fold (step 12–17) to lock the back. Carefully curving the back, inside edges of the wings can help keep the lock closed, reduce drag and increase lift.

1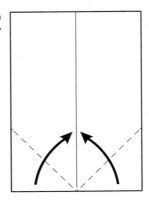

Begin with the back side up, in vertical orientation. Fold and unfold along the center line.

2

Fold the bottom edges to the center.

3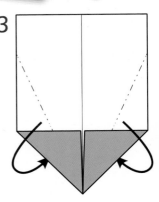

Mountain fold the bottom edges to the center line without creasing the triangular flaps.

4

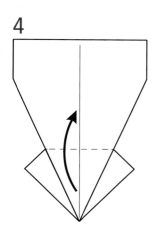

Valley fold up at the narrowest width.

5

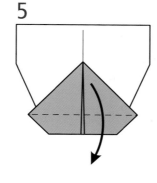

Valley fold down at the widest point.

6

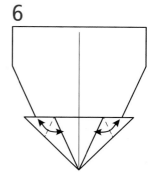

Fold down the corners. Unfold.

7

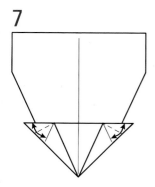

Fold down to the previous creases. Unfold.

8

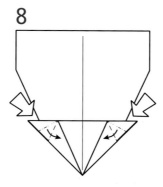

Squash fold both sides.

9

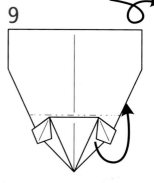

Mountain fold the entire nose behind. Turn over.

10

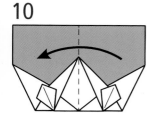

Valley fold in half.

11

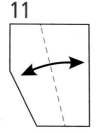

Valley fold the top edge of wing to the bottom of the plane. Unfold.

12

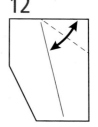

Fold the back edge to the base of the wing. Unfold.

13

Fold the back edge to the previous crease. Unfold.

14

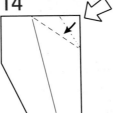

Squash fold.

15

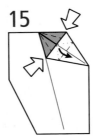

Fold the edge down, and squash the sides to form a Frog Fold.

16

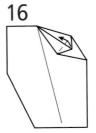

Fold the point up.

17

Mountain fold around to complete the lock.

18

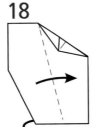

Fold the wings out.

19

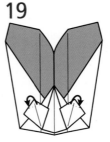

Mountain fold the tips of the nose, and tuck them under lower layers to reduce drag.

20

Adjust the wings and fly.

The Fireball

In Western mythology, dragons often possess the ability to breathe fire, which makes them all the more fearsome. However, exactly how they do this never seems to be explained. This Fireball is a handy accessory for any dragon that prefers its food well done.

Dragon Mastery Tip: The front portion of The Fireball is called a *canard*, in paper plane terms. Be sure to adjust it for symmetry. If set at a slightly lesser angle than the wings, it can provide added stability in flight.

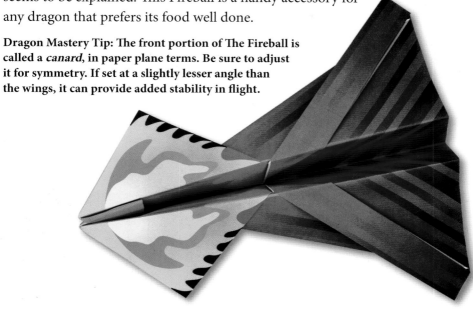

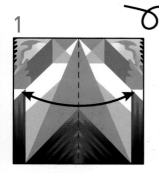

1

Begin with the front side up. Valley fold edge to edge. Unfold. Turn over.

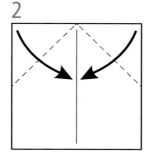

2

Fold the top edges to the center crease.

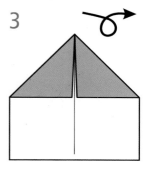

3

Turn over.

4

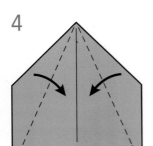

Fold the top edges to the center. Be sure not to fold the lower layer.

5

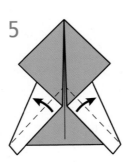

Fold the edges outward.

6

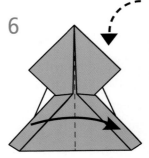

Valley fold in half. Rotate 90°.

7

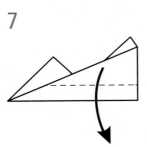

Valley fold down.

8

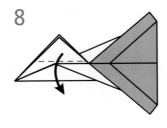

Fold down along the edge.

9

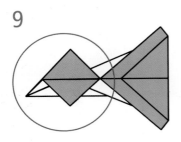

Zoom In.

10

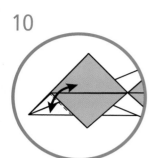

Fold and unfold along the edge.

11

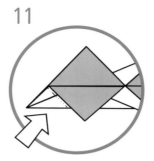

Inside reverse fold.

12

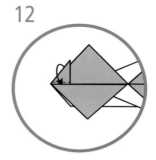

Valley fold and tuck the flap in.

13

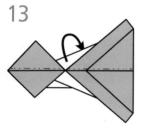

Fold down the other wing to match. Adjust and fly.

The Mini Dragon

The Mini Dragon is by far the cutest, friendliest dragon. It is the sort that would befriend a small child, and let her ride home on its back. Its wide, high-mounted wings, and c-shaped winglets give it a stable, easy flying style. A bit like a hang glider.

Dragon Mastery Tip: Be sure to fold both sides of the head back firmly, to avoid excess drag.

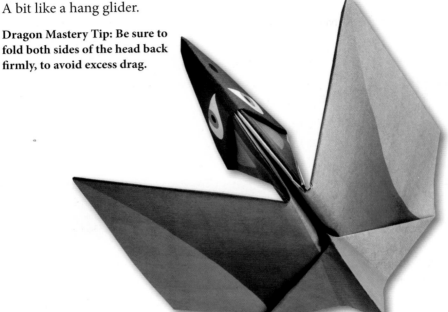

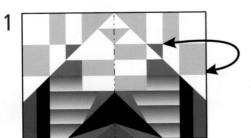

1

Begin with the back side up, in horizontal orientation. Mountain fold and unfold, edge to edge.

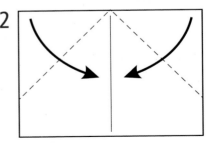

2

Fold the top edges in to the center.

3

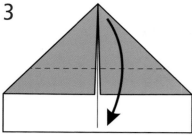

Fold down the top corner to the bottom edge.

4

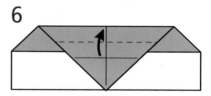

Valley fold the corner up to the top edge.

5

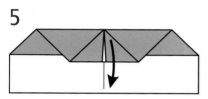

Unfold.

6

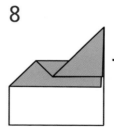

Fold the crease up to align with the top edge.

7

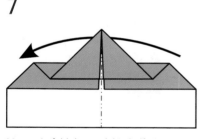

Mountain fold the model in half.

8

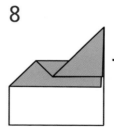

Rotate 90°.

9

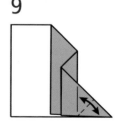

Fold the bottom edge of the triangle up to match the crease. Unfold.

10

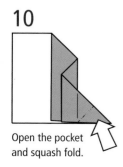

Open the pocket and squash fold.

11

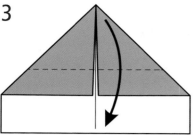

The squash fold in progress.

12

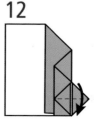

Fold the top flap down.

13

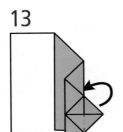

Firmly mountain fold the head in half.

14

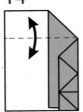

Fold the top edge down to match the diagonal edges. Unfold.

15

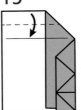

Fold the top edge down to the crease.

16

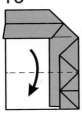

Fold the wing down.

17

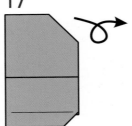

Turn over.

18

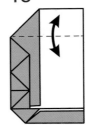

Fold the top edge down to match the diagonal edges. Unfold.

19

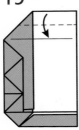

Fold the top edge down to the crease.

20

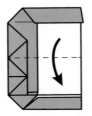

Fold the wing down.

21

Fold both wings up.

22

Valley fold the bottom edge up diagonally to line up with the outside of the head. Unfold.

23

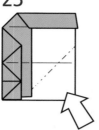

Reverse fold along the crease.

24

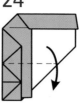

Fold the wing down. The tail opens up.

25

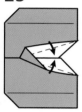

Valley fold along the diagonals from the front of the tail to the back corners.

26

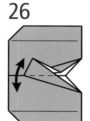

Fold the remaining paper back and forth, and make it stand straight. This is called a Rabbit Ear fold. Adjust the wings, and straighten up the body.

27

Front view. The Mini Dragon is finished.

The Fighter Dragon

The Fighter Dragon is a horned robot dinosaur combined with a war plane. Needless to say, this monstrosity was the ill-conceived result of a mad scientist's vanity project—The last, before his division's funding was inevitably cut.

Dragon Mastery Tip: Unlike the other dragon planes in this kit, this one requires a cut (step 8). The cut can be made with scissors or a sharp knife. Many other paper planes use a similar cut to create a tail fin.

1

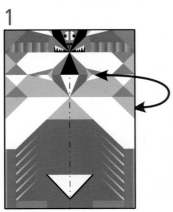

Begin with the front side up, in vertical orientation. Mountain fold edge to edge. Unfold.

2

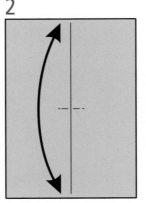

Pinch fold to mark the center.

3

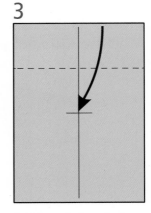

Fold down the top edge to the pinch mark.

4

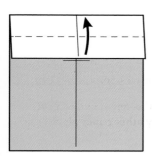

Fold the edge to the top.

5

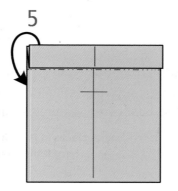

Mountain fold the top strip backward along its bottom edge.

6

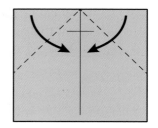

Valley fold the top edges to the center line, folding through all layers.

7

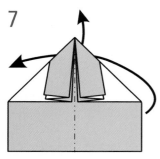

Mountain fold in half and pull up the flap.

8

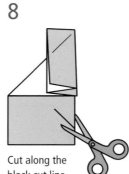

Cut along the black cut line.

9

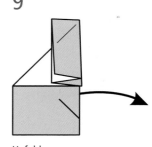

Unfold.

10

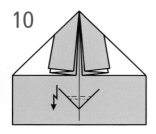

Crimp fold back and forth to form the foot.

11

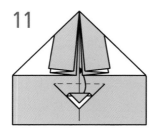

Valley fold the flap up, tucking it under all layers.

12

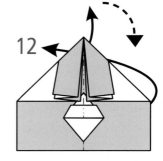

Mountain fold the model in half and pull up the flap. Rotate 90°.

13

Fold the corner to the bottom edge. Unfold.

14

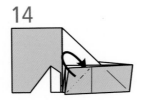

Mountain fold and tuck the flap in.

15

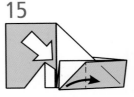

Valley fold the flap forward, and squash fold the triangle.

16

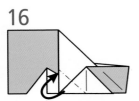

Mountain fold the corner inside.

17

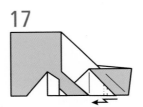

Crimp fold to form the foot.

18

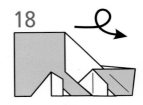

Turn over.

19

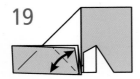

Repeat 13–17 on this side. Fold the corner to the bottom edge. Unfold.

20

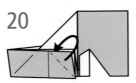

Mountain fold and tuck the flap in.

21

Valley fold the flap forward, and squash fold the triangle.

22

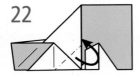

Mountain fold the corner inside.

23

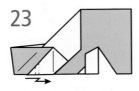

Crimp fold to form the foot.

24

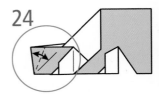

Fold to the crease line. Unfold.

25

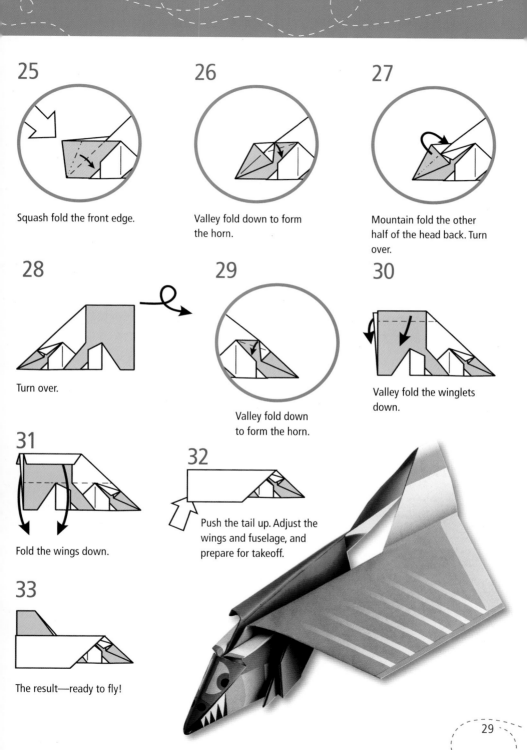

Squash fold the front edge.

26

Valley fold down to form
the horn.

27

Mountain fold the other
half of the head back. Turn
over.

28

Turn over.

29

Valley fold down
to form the horn.

30

Valley fold the winglets
down.

31

Fold the wings down.

32

Push the tail up. Adjust the
wings and fuselage, and
prepare for takeoff.

33

The result—ready to fly!

The Gargoyle

When they are not busy guarding castles, gargoyles are known for their terrifying claws that they use to hunt prey; this dragon can be seen circling the skies, looking for its next meal. They are capable of snatching intruders and flying away with them. You can perch this dragon anywhere you need it to keep an eye on things. It actually flies much better than the ones made of stone.

Dragon Mastery Tip: Take care to adjust the flaps forming the claws. Both flaps should be adjusted to the same angle. Adding a paperclip or small weight to the nose will increase flight distances. Also, be sure to crease the body firmly, so it will stay closed.

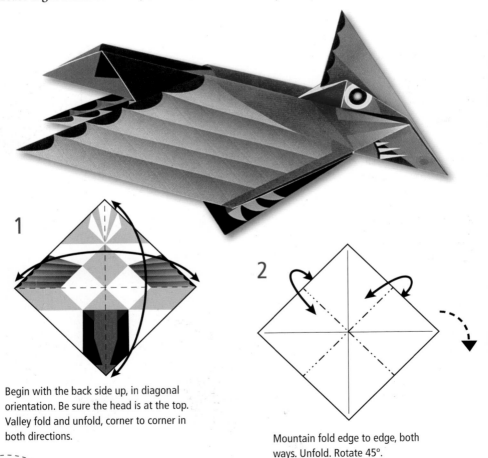

1 Begin with the back side up, in diagonal orientation. Be sure the head is at the top. Valley fold and unfold, corner to corner in both directions.

2 Mountain fold edge to edge, both ways. Unfold. Rotate 45°.

3

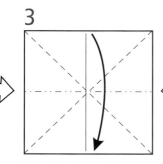

Bring the edges to the center using the existing creases.

4

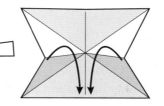

In progress. Note the raised corners meeting at the bottom center.

5

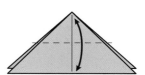

Fold in half through both layers. Unfold.

6

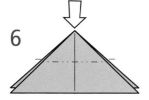

Open the paper to form a pyramid and gently push in the tip to coax it to invert. This operation is called an "open sink." Refold the paper to look like diagram 7.

7

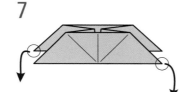

Pull downward on the two opposite corners.

8

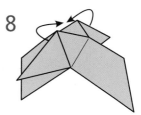

In progress. Note the top corners coming together. Coax them to assume the form shown in diagram 9.

9

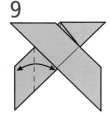

Fold the edge to the center and crease firmly. Unfold.

10

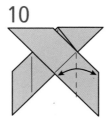

Repeat on the other side.

11

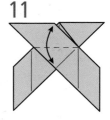

Fold down at the narrowest point, folding through all layers. Unfold.

12

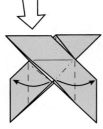

Using the existing creases, open the flap and bring the top corner down along the center.

13

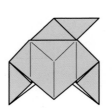

Turn over.

14

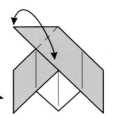

Valley fold. Unfold.

15

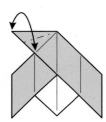

Mountain fold to crease. Unfold.

16

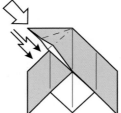

Pleat both layers.

17

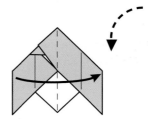

Valley fold in half along the center. Rotate 90°.

18

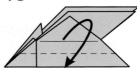

Valley fold the front wing down, so this crease aligns with the bottom edge.

19

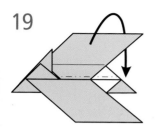

Mountain fold the rear wing down to match.

20

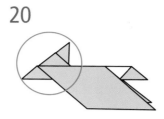

Zoom in.

21

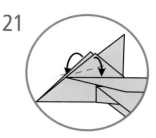

Valley fold the corner to create the eye. Repeat on the back.

22

Make final adjustments. Lower the claws. Prepare to fly.

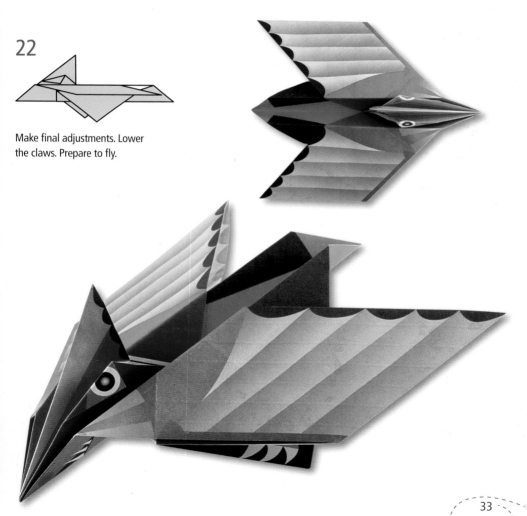

The Swoop Dragon

Known for their aerial acrobatics, swooping dragons are fearsome creatures that rule the skies. The Swoop Dragon is folded from a single square sheet of paper and can perform death-defying feats and aerial loops. Be very careful near a Swoop Dragon, even when raised as pets they have been known to turn on their masters, forcing them to dive for cover!

Dragon Mastery Tip: Opening or closing the pockets on each wingtip will cause your swoop dragon to glide or loop. Try it both ways.

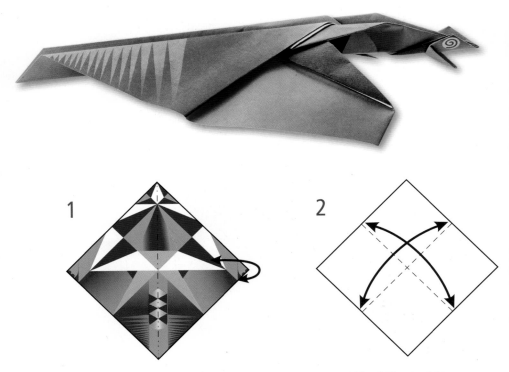

1

Begin with the back side up, in diagonal orientation. Be sure the head is at the top. Mountain fold the side corner to the opposite corner. Unfold.

2

Valley fold and unfold, edge to edge.

3

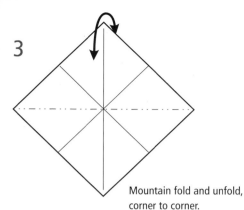

Mountain fold and unfold, corner to corner.

4

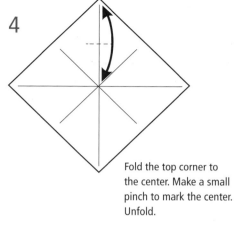

Fold the top corner to the center. Make a small pinch to mark the center. Unfold.

5

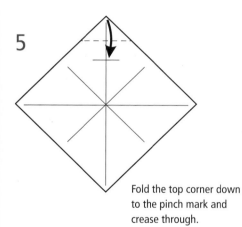

Fold the top corner down to the pinch mark and crease through.

6

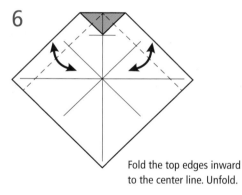

Fold the top edges inward to the center line. Unfold.

7

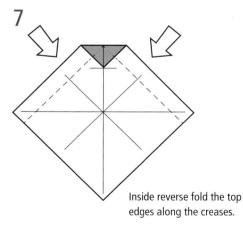

Inside reverse fold the top edges along the creases.

8

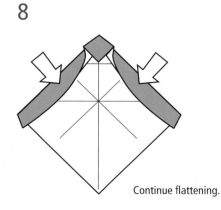

Continue flattening.

9 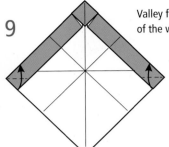 Valley fold the corners of the wings up.

10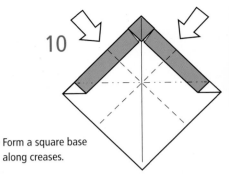

Form a square base along creases.

11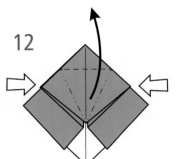

Fold the edges to the center. Unfold.

12

Petal fold, being careful not to trap the square flaps created in step 7.

13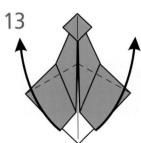

Valley fold the wings upward.

14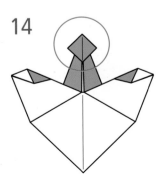

Zoom in.

15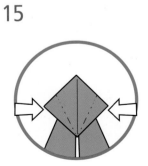

Inside reverse fold the edges to the center.

16

Valley fold the flap up to form the mouth.

17

Zoom out.

18

Mountain fold in half along the center.

19

Rotate 90°.

20

Fold the wings down from the base of the head to the end of the wings. Adjust, and prepare to launch.

Throw the dragon straight up, with its wings angled downward. It will fly back to you!

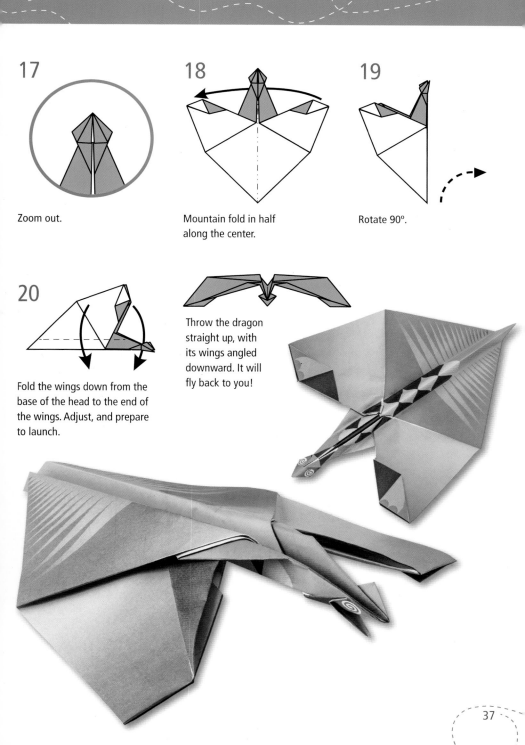

The Flying Demon

The Flying Demon is the scariest dragon. Demons in folklore come in various forms. This one has an angular body, sharp claws and a heavy head, which allows you to throw it firmly. The Flying Demon is folded from a square sheet. Its head is formed from an offset square, making it a distant relative of the Swoop Dragon, Flying Shark and Flame Monster. The folding is fairly straight-forward, but it may help to review the instructions on the petal, swivel and inside reverse fold.

Dragon Mastery Tip: The Flying Demon is a fairly small, solid dragon. Its claws serve as winglets, stabilizing its flight. Its body does not lock, so you will need to fold it firmly, and angle the wings upward. It should achieve good distance, with a firm throw.

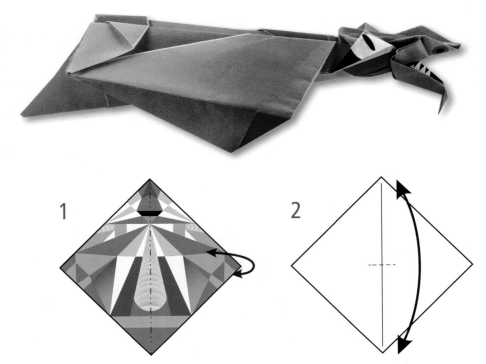

1

Begin with the back side up, in diagonal orientation. Be sure the head is at the top. Mountain fold and unfold, corner to corner.

2

Fold the top corner to the bottom. Make a small pinch to mark the center. Unfold.

3

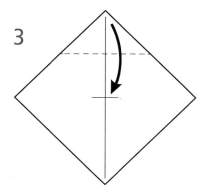

Fold the top corner down to the pinch mark.

4

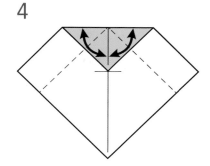

Fold the top edges inward to the center line. Unfold.

5

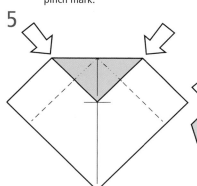

Inside reverse fold the top edges along the creases.

6

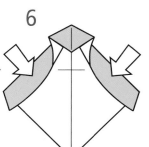

Continue flattening.

7

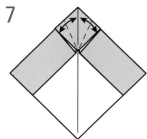

Valley fold the bottom edges of the square to the center line. Unfold.

8

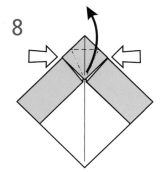

Pull up the bottom corner, and push in the side corners to complete the Petal Fold.

9

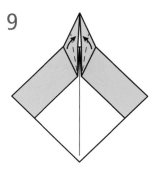

Valley fold the bottom edges to the center.

10

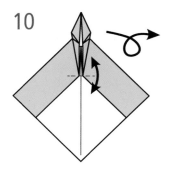

Pinch fold at the bottom of the points. Unfold. Turn over.

11

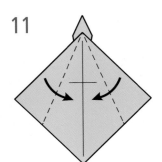

Valley fold the top edges to the center.

12

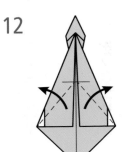

The pinch fold from step 9 is under the flaps. From the pinch, fold them out to their bottom corners.

13

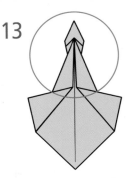

Zoom in.

14

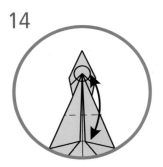

Valley fold this point down to the inside corners of the wings. Unfold.

15

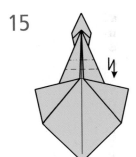

Mountain fold the crease you made in step 13, and fold it down to the corners, forming a crimp.

16

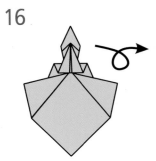

Turn over.

17

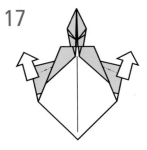

Pull the top layer of each wing up as far as it will go. Swivel fold from the center.

18

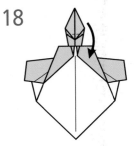

Valley fold the top flap down.

19

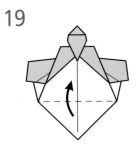

Fold the bottom corner up from the base of the wings.

20

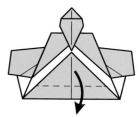

Fold downward to form the tail.

21

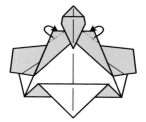

Mountain fold the top corners back to form the eyes.

22

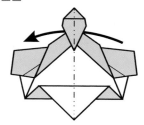

Mountain fold the model in half.

23

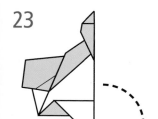

Rotate 90°.

24

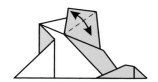

Valley fold the wing tips downward. Unfold.

25

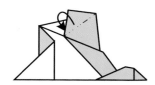

Reverse the folds, and tuck the flap in.

26

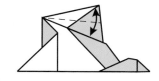

Fold the top of wing to the inside edge. Unfold.

27

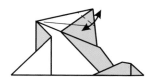

Fold the closed edge to the crease. Unfold.

28

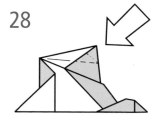

Squash fold.

29

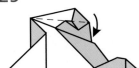

Fold down along the crease.

30

Turn over.

31

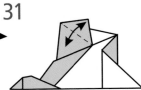

Repeat steps 23–28 on the other side: Fold the top of the wing to the inside edge. Unfold.

32

Reverse the fold, and tuck the flap in.

33

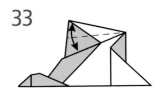

Fold down along the crease. Unfold.

34

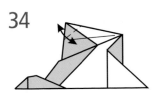

Fold the closed edge to the crease. Unfold.

35

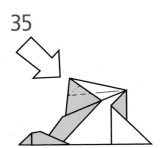

Squash fold.

36

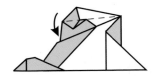

Valley fold the wing tips downward.

37

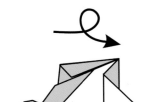

Turn over.

38

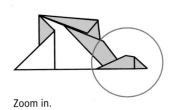

Zoom in.

39

Pull the corner down, and reverse them to form the mouth.

40

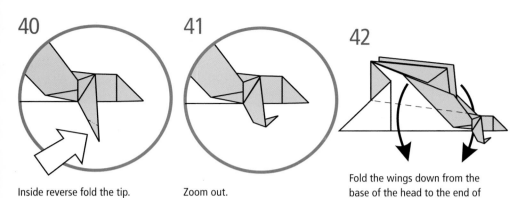

Inside reverse fold the tip.

41

Zoom out.

42

Fold the wings down from the base of the head to the end of the wings. Adjust, and prepare to launch.

43

The Flying Demon is finished.

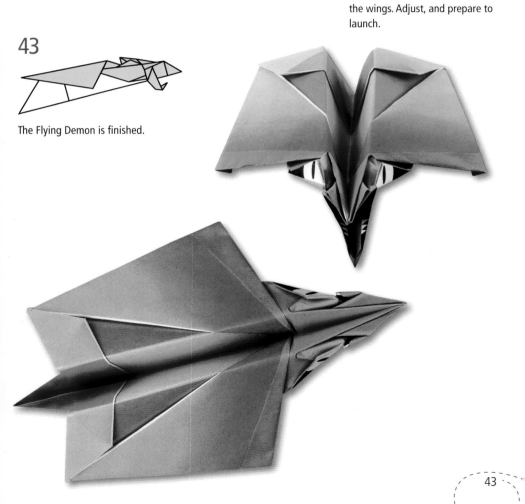

The Insectoid Dragon

A fearsome four-winged dragon that darts through the air, changing direction in the blink of an eye. Imagine a snapping turtle in the body of a dragonfly. The more you think about it, the scarier this one is!

Dragon Mastery Tip: Evenly spacing the four wings will give the best flight. Also make sure the tail fins are not misaligned.

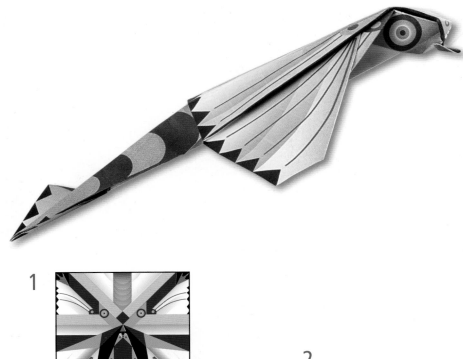

1

Cut the tail portion of the sheet. Discard the white strip.

2

Begin with the tail portion. Valley fold in half from edge to edge. Unfold.

3

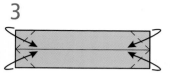

Valley fold all four corners to the center crease.

4

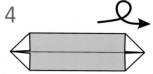

Turn over.

5

Valley fold the new edges to the center crease, through the top layer only.

6

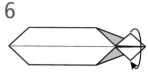

Fold the flap down.

7

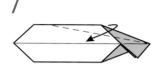

Valley fold the new edge to the center crease.

8

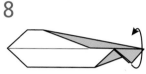

Fold the top layer of the tail flap back up.

9

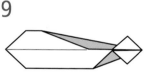

Repeat steps 6–8 on the bottom half.

10

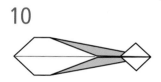

The finished tail.

11

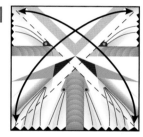

Retrieve the square portion. Begin with the back side facing up. Valley fold the opposite corners together. Unfold.

12

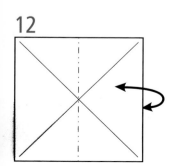

Mountain fold in half. Unfold.

13

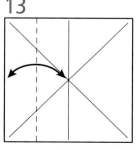

Valley fold to the center line. Unfold.

14

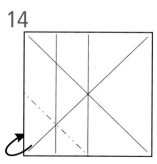

Mountain fold the bottom left corner to the center.

15

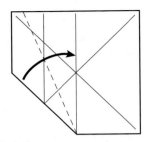

Fold the edge from the previous step to the center.

16

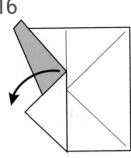

Unfold.

17

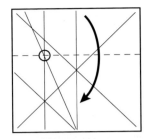

Find the circled intersection. Valley fold down along this point.

18

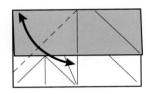

Fold the top edge to the center. Unfold.

19

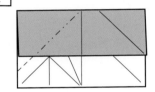

Inside reverse fold along this crease.

20

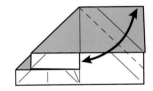

Fold the top edge to the center. Unfold.

21

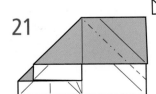

Inside reverse fold along this crease.

22

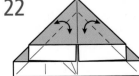

Crease through the top layers. The body is formed. Now we add the tail.

23

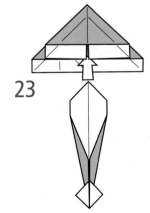

Insert the tail between the layers, as far as it can go.

24

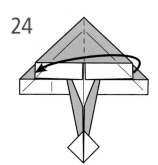

Fold the bottom wing over.

25

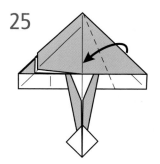

Valley fold the edge of the wing to the center line.

26

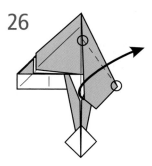

Valley fold the edge of the wing outward.

27

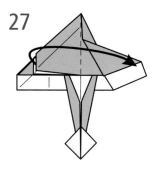

Valley fold two flaps over.

28

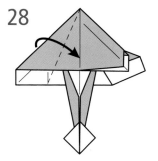

Valley fold the edge of the wing to the center line.

29

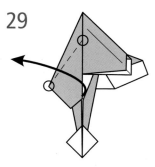

Valley fold the edge of the wing outward.

30

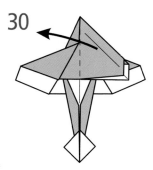

Return the top flap to the left.

31

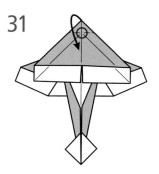

Valley fold the nose inward. Use the intersecting creases as a reference.

32

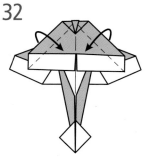

Using the existing creases, reverse fold the edges of the smaller wings under the tip of the nose.

33

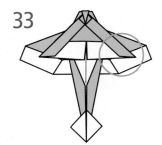

Zoom in to fold the claw.

34

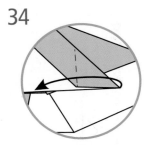

Valley fold the claw inward at a right angle to the wing edge.

35

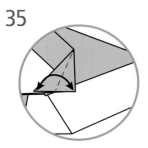

Valley fold the flap in half. Unfold.

36

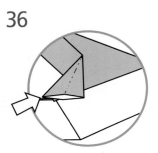

Squash the flap to flatten the claw.

37

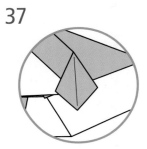

The finished claw. Zoom out.

38

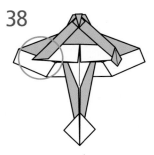

Zoom in. We will repeat 34–37 on the opposite side.

39

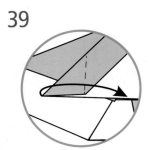

Valley fold the **claw inward at** a right angle to **the wing edge.**

40

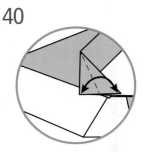

Valley fold the flap in half. Unfold.

41

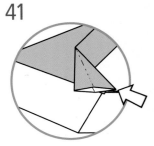

Squash the flap to flatten the claw.

42

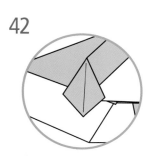

The finished claw. Zoom out.

43

Zoom in on the head to finish the mouth.

44

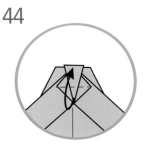

Valley fold the flap to the tip of the nose to form the mouth.

45

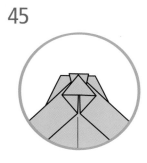

The finished mouth. Zoom out.

46

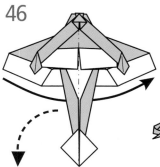

Mountain fold in half to finish the dragon. Rotate 90°.

47

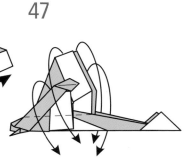

Fold all wings down, from the base of the head to the end of the wings. Adjust, and prepare to launch.

48

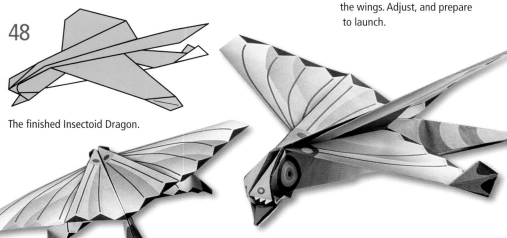

The finished Insectoid Dragon.

The Flying Shark

The Flying Shark is a graceful predator patrolling the skies. Its name comes from the way it effortlessly glides through the air, as if it were water. Imagine menacing music playing at an increasing volume as this silent killer sneaks up on an unsuspecting target.

Dragon Mastery Tip: Throw your Flying Shark with the wings parallel to the ground or at a slight upward angle for best gliding.

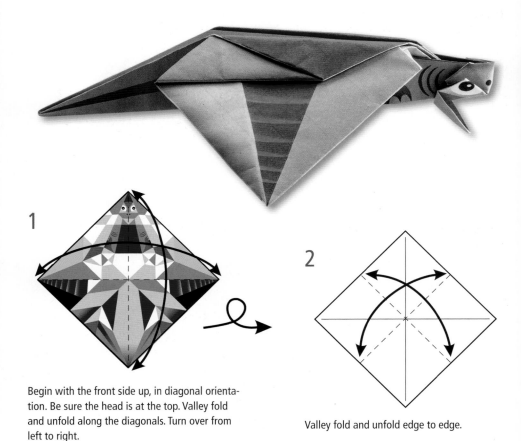

1

Begin with the front side up, in diagonal orientation. Be sure the head is at the top. Valley fold and unfold along the diagonals. Turn over from left to right.

2

Valley fold and unfold edge to edge.

3

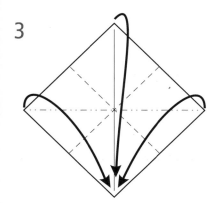

Make a Square Base by pulling all corners to the bottom along the existing creases.

4

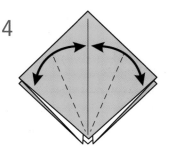

Fold and unfold the bottom edges to the center. Fold through two layers. Unfold.

5

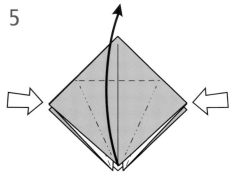

Petal fold along the creases created in the previous step.

6

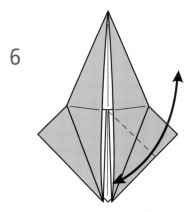

Fold along the bottom edge. Unfold.

7   8   9

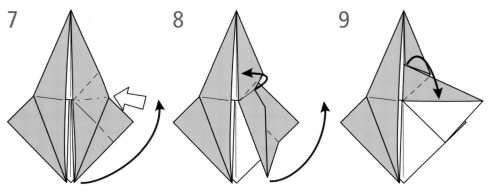

Swivel fold on the crease created in the previous step.

Step 7 in progress.

Valley fold the flap down.

10

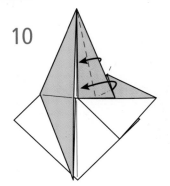

Fold the edge to the center line. Swivel fold lower layer, and then flatten.

11

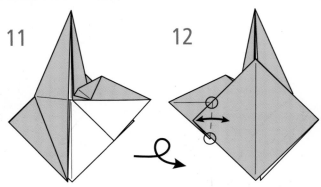

Turn over.

12

Valley fold from the corner to the end of the crease on the wing. Unfold.

13

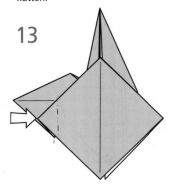

Inside reverse fold along the crease from the previous step.

14

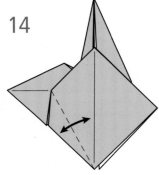

Valley fold the edge to the center. Unfold.

15

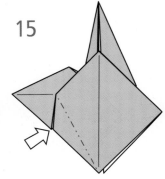

Inside reverse fold using the crease from the previous step.

16

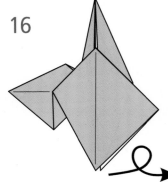

Turn over.

17

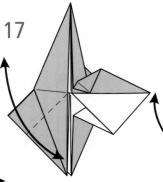

Repeat steps 6–15 to form the other wing: Fold along the bottom edge. Unfold.

18

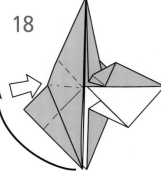

Swivel fold on the crease created in the previous step.

19

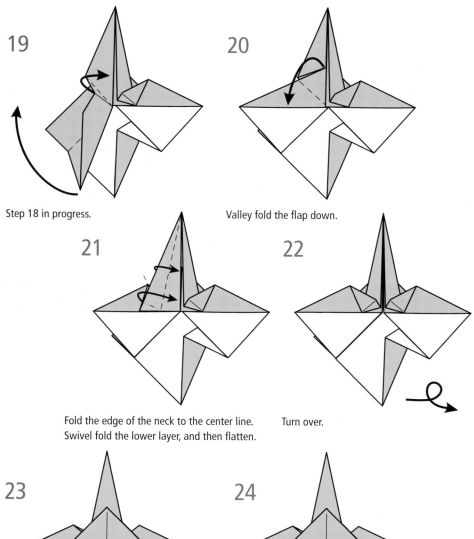

Step 18 in progress.

20

Valley fold the flap down.

21

Fold the edge of the neck to the center line.
Swivel fold the lower layer, and then flatten.

22

Turn over.

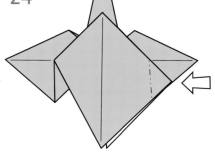

23

Valley fold from the corner to the end of
the crease on the wing. Unfold.

24

Inside reverse fold using the crease from
the previous step.

25

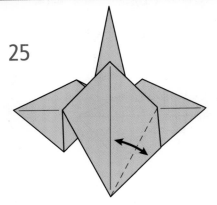

Valley fold the edge to the center. Unfold.

26

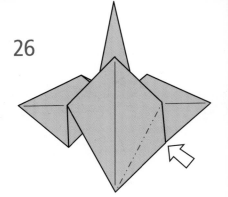

Inside reverse fold using the crease from the previous step.

27

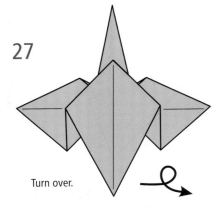

Turn over.

28

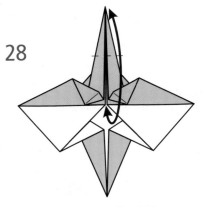

Valley fold the neck in half. Unfold.

29

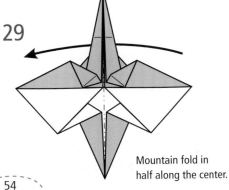

Mountain fold in half along the center.

30

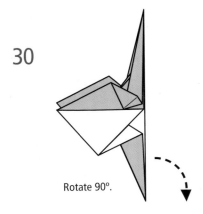

Rotate 90°.

31

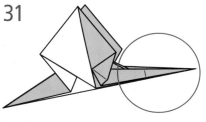

Zoom in.

32

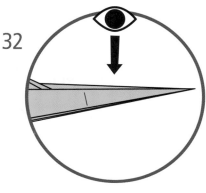

View from the top.

33

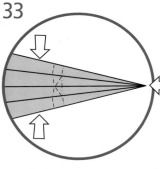

Open the layers of the head and squeeze the layers together where the crease was made in step 28.

34

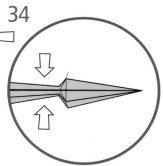

The center 2 sections stay spread as the collapse continues.

35

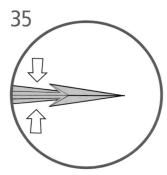

As the collapse finishes the head will flatten. Side view.

36

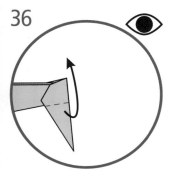

View from the side. Valley fold through both layers along the edge of the neck.

37

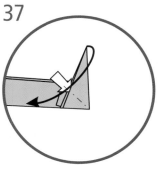

Open the flap and squash fold.

38

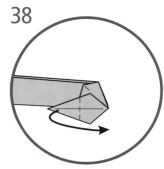

Valley fold the mouth forward.

39

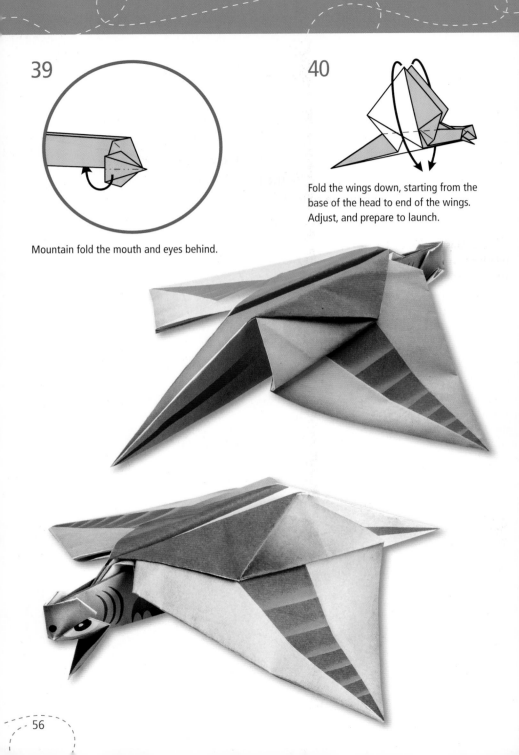

Mountain fold the mouth and eyes behind.

40

Fold the wings down, starting from the base of the head to end of the wings. Adjust, and prepare to launch.

The Flame Monster

The Flame Monster is a very well-articulated dragon. You may notice that it shares some features of the iconic origami crane. Mother Flame Monsters lay their eggs in volcanoes. The eggs hatch when the volcano erupts. Flame Monsters are very dangerous, despite their small stature. They attack in large swarms, much like an airborne school of fire-breathing piranhas. These dragons love fire, and hate water.

Dragon Mastery Tip: Like the chicken, the Flame monster suffers from a heavy body and relatively small wings, limiting its gliding ability. It will need to rely mostly on the force of your throw for flight. Try to get it to land on its feet.

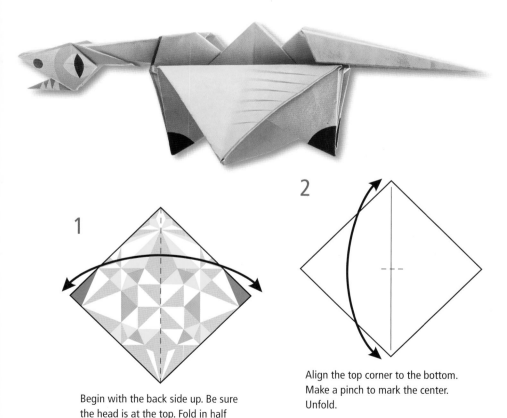

1

Begin with the back side up. Be sure the head is at the top. Fold in half vertically. Unfold.

2

Align the top corner to the bottom. Make a pinch to mark the center. Unfold.

3

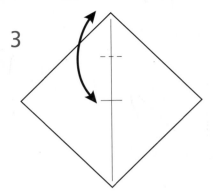

Align the top corner to the center. Make a pinch mark. Unfold.

4

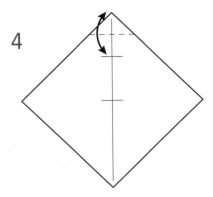

Fold the top corner down to the previous pinch. Unfold.

5

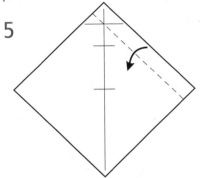

Valley fold the outside edge through the intersection where the top fold meets the center crease.

6

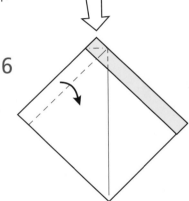

Fold the other edge in. Mountain fold through the center of the top portion. Push the top point to the right side. This forms a Rabbit Ear fold.

7

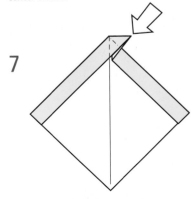

Squash fold the Rabbit Ear to form a square.

8

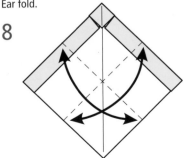

Fold and unfold edge to edge, through the center, in both directions.

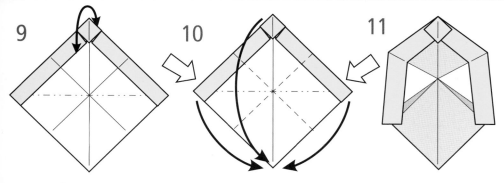

9

10

11

Mountain fold the bottom corner up to the top. Unfold.

Push in the side corners, and move the top corner down to collapse.

The collapse in progress.

12

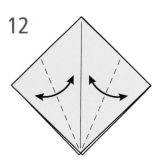

The collapse is complete. Fold the bottom edges to the center. Unfold.

13

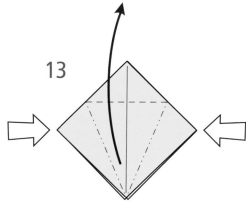

Petal fold the top flap.

14

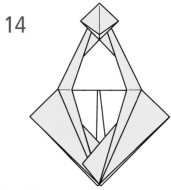

Step 13 in progress.

15

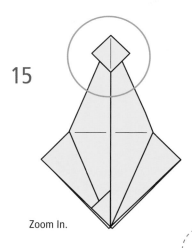

Zoom In.

16

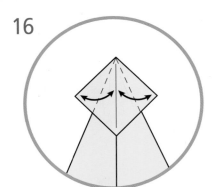

Fold the top edges to the center. Unfold.

17

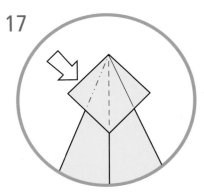

Squash fold.

18

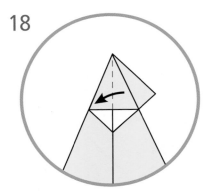

Valley fold the flap over.

19

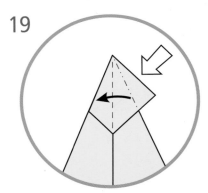

Squash fold the other side.

20

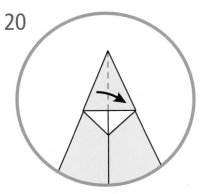

Fold the flap over, leaving two layers on each side.

21

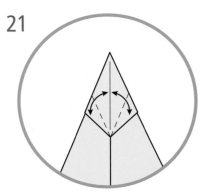

Valley fold the lower edges to the center. Unfold.

22

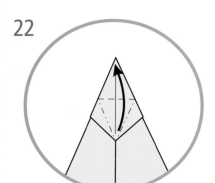

Fold the bottom corner to the top, and reverse the creases to mountain folds, to complete the Frog Fold.

23

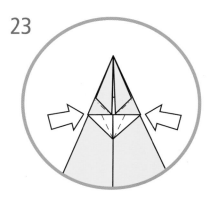

Inside reverse fold both sides.

24

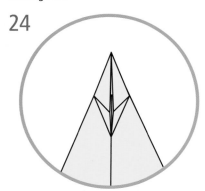

Zoom out.

25

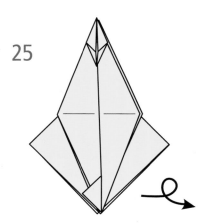

Turn over.

26

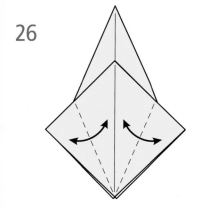

Fold the bottom edges to the center. Unfold.

27

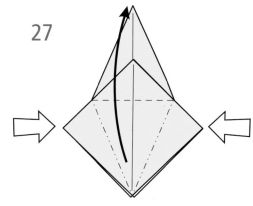

Petal fold.

28

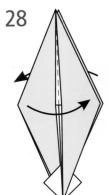

Valley fold the left flap on the front and the right flap on the rear to turn the model inside out.

29

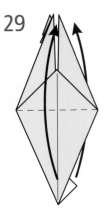

Fold the wings up.

30

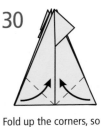

Fold up the corners, so the bottom edges fall on the center line.

31

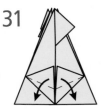

Fold the corners down.

32

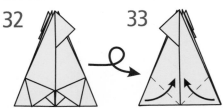

Turn over.

33

Fold up the corners so the bottom edges fall on the center line.

34

Fold the corners down.

35

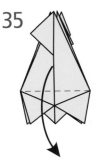

Fold the front wing down.

36

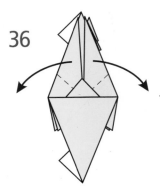

Valley fold down the head and tail along the top edge of the wings.

37

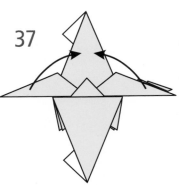

Unfold.

38

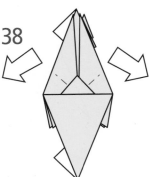

Inside reverse fold the head and tail along the previous creases.

39

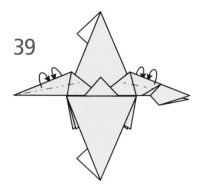

Thin the head and tail by mountain folding inward on both sides.

40

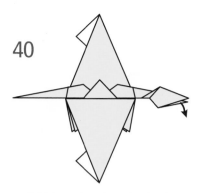

Fold down the other wing, level, and open the bottom jaw. The Flame Monster is ready to fly.

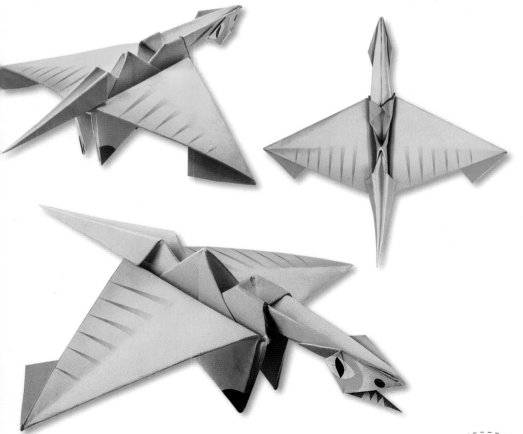

About the Authors

Sam Ita began his fascination with paper airplanes at an early age. He started as a production assistant for Robert Sabuda and Mathew Reinhart, and worked on many bestselling pop-up books. His creations include *Christmas Tree In-a-Box*, *Van Gogh's Sunflowers In-a-Box*, *The Odyssey*, *Moby Dick*, *20,000 Leagues Under the Sea* and *Frankenstein*. Sam lives in New York.

Paul Frasco is a New York-based origami designer focused on expressive animal and fantasy designs boasting fun and accessible folding sequences. He has been featured in public spaces, museums, libraries and galleries around the US. Paul co-authored *Creative Origami and Beyond*.